THE SPIRAL OF REMEMBERING

"You do not need to become more.
You need only to remember who you are,
allow what is already within you to rise,
and trust the spiral as it brings you home."
— *The Spiral of Remembering*

THE SPIRAL OF REMEMBERING

A JOURNEY HOME
TO THE SELF

DAWN SMITH

This book is a living transmission.
It was not written to be owned,
but to be remembered.

It is offered in love, in Light,
and in the hope that it awakens
something ancient and true within you.

You are welcome to quote its passages,
whisper them to the wind,
or read them aloud under moonlight —
so long as you do so with integrity,
and with reverence for the heart from which they came.

This creation was not planned...
it was revealed.

Not copyrighted —
but protected by the Light it carries.

If these words found you,
trust that it was time.
And may you carry their Light forward
in your own sacred way.

Dedication

For the one who is awakening.
For the one who has always known.
For the one whose breath carries ancient remembering.

This is not just a book.
It is a mirror.
A doorway.
A quiet return.

It is for the seeker who paused mid-step...
the dreamer who doubted...
the Lightbearer who forgot their own glow —
but never stopped reaching for it.

It is for the one who chose to stay.
To soften.
To listen.
To come home.

This is not a beginning.
This is a remembering.

And you, Beloved...
You are the embodiment of Light itself.
The frequency remembered.
The spiral, walking.
You are the one this was always for.

You are not late.
You are not lost.
You are here.

And now... *you remember.*

Table of Contents

How to Use This Book

This is not a book to read once.
It's a companion. A spiral.
A sacred space for your own remembering.

There is no right way to move through these pages.
You are invited to follow your intuition.
Let your breath guide you.
Let yourSelf speak through the margins.

Each section offers:

✧ A conversation between the Human and the Self

✧ A theme to explore — like Worthiness, Trust, or Receiving

✧ A mantra or whisper to anchor the energy

✧ Reflection pages to journal what rises within you

This book isn't complete without *you.*
Your insights. Your presence. Your truth.

Here are a few ways to co-create with it:

✧ Write in the margins. Circle words.
Let the pages carry your fingerprints.

✧ Use a pen you love — one that feels like an extension of
yourSelf.

✧ Pause between sections. Breathe. Walk.
Come back when you're ready.

✧ Return to the same prompt more than once — your
answers will shift as you do.

✧ Read aloud to yourSelf — your voice carries power.

✧ Mark the pages that feel like home.

This is a conversation — not just between words and reader,
but between **you and your own inner knowing.**

Some days, one line will be enough.
Some days, the blank page will be your sanctuary.
All of it is sacred. All of it is enough.

> *"I am not just reading...*
> *I am remembering."*

Acknowledgments

To the Light within me —
thank you for never giving up on being seen.
For whispering, even when I wasn't listening.
For waiting, even when I wandered.
For reminding me that home is not a place — it's a presence.

To the sacred stillness where truth speaks clearly —
thank you for always welcoming me back.
You are the breath I didn't know I was holding.
The space where I remember.
The silence that says, *I never left you.*

To every version of me — the one who searched, who forgot,
who doubted, who dared...thank you.
You carried the spark.
You kept walking.
You led me here.

To those whose presence supported this unfolding — seen
and unseen, near and far...
Your love is woven into every word, every pause, every pulse
of Light on these pages.

And to you, dear reader —
You were never just reading.
You were remembering.
You were awakening the voice that was always yours.
This was always for you.
Your remembrance ripples into eternity.

May this meet you in the moment you choose yourSelf —
and may that choice feel like coming home.
Again. And again. And again.

The Moment You Choose You

Human: I've spent so long trying to be who I thought I needed to be... for others, for approval, for safety. But none of it feels like me anymore.

Self: That is the beginning. When the pretending begins to crumble, the remembering can begin. The moment you choose you — authentically, unapologetically — is the moment your true life begins.

Human: But it feels uncertain. Like I don't know who I am without all the roles I've been playing.

Self: That's okay. You don't need all the answers. You only need one truth to begin: You are worth choosing.
Not someday. Not when you're better. *Now.*

Human: What if others don't understand this choice?

Self: Then it's an opportunity to honor your truth even more deeply. Choosing yourSelf may stir discomfort in others. Let it. It's not rejection — it's redirection. The ones who are meant to walk with you will feel the resonance of your truth.

Human: So I don't have to wait to be perfect to begin?

Self: No. You begin from where you are. That's the power of choice. And every time you choose yourSelf again, the path reveals more of who you truly are.

Human: I'm choosing me now... even if I'm not sure what comes next.

Self: That's the most powerful choice of all.

I am simply the mirror...
reflecting you back to yourSelf.

What does yourSelf want you to remember?

_____

_____

_____

_____

_____

_____

_____

_____

_____

_____

_____

_____

_____

_____

_____

_____

_____

_____

_____

_____

_____

_____

_____

Worthiness

Human: I've tried to earn my worth through doing, proving, pleasing... but it always feels temporary. Always feeling like I can lose it.

Self: Because what you were chasing wasn't real worth — it was approval. Worthiness is not something to be earned. It is your origin. Your essence. It cannot be increased or diminished.

Human: But I still feel not enough sometimes.

Self: That's the echo of forgetting. The remnants of conditioning. Your worth was never in question — but your belief in it was. Now, you are remembering.

Human: What helps me remember?

Self: Gentleness. Presence. Choosing yourSelf again and again. Speaking to yourSelf with love. Letting go of comparison. Letting in compassion.

Human: I want to believe I am worthy.

Self: Then treat yourSelf as though you already are. Worthiness is not a feeling to chase — it is a frequency to live from. The more you honor it, the more it roots into your being.

Human: So I don't have to do anything to deserve it?

Self: No. You only have to be. You are worthy because you exist.

You are worthy.
You are complete.

What is yourSelf whispering today?

Receiving

Human: I'm learning to ask for what I need... but I still struggle to receive it. A part of me feels unworthy or unsure.

Self: Receiving begins with openness, not just in what we do, but in how we *be*. It's the quiet art of letting life reach us... of whispering, *"Yes, I'm ready to allow in what's meant for me."*

Human: So I've been blocking the very things I ask for?

Self: Sometimes, yes. Not intentionally. But your energy must match your desire. Receiving is a surrender, not a striving. It's the frequency of *"I am safe to allow."*

Human: How do I shift into that space?

Self: Begin with gratitude. Practice presence. Notice what you do receive — kindness, beauty, breath. Let life reflect your worth through the support already all around you. The more you notice it, the more trust becomes your natural state.

Human: What about when I receive something and feel guilty?

Self: Then meet the guilt with compassion, not judgment. Guilt is often an old voice — one that says you must earn everything. But love, grace, abundance... these are not earned. They are remembered.

Human: I want to feel open.

Self: Then practice saying *yes*. Even silently. Even softly. Receive a compliment. Receive rest. Receive beauty. And know that in doing so... you are receiving *you*.

Breathe. Listen. Remember.

What would yourSelf like you to remember?

_____

_____

_____

_____

_____

_____

_____

_____

_____

_____

_____

_____

_____

_____

_____

_____

_____

_____

_____

_____

_____

Abundance

Human: I've longed for abundance, but I often feel like there's not enough. Not enough time, support, resources... sometimes even love.

Self: Abundance is not just what you have — it's what you believe you have access to. It begins within. When you see yourSelf as connected to the infinite, lack begins to dissolve.

Human: But what about the real limitations I face?

Self: Limitations may feel real — but they are not **absolute.** They are not the final truth. They are reflections — of beliefs, patterns, energies, and habits once accepted as reality. They are real experiences, but not your ultimate identity.

Human: What does that frequency feel like?

Self: Trust. Openness. Gratitude. Flow. It's not about having everything now—it's about knowing that more is always on its way, because you are connected to the Source of All.

Human: So I don't have to force it?

Self: No. You allow in the quiet knowing... *what I have is enough.* You give from overflow — never from depletion or duty. You receive without guilt, without apology. You begin to speak to money, time, and love as sacred allies — not enemies. Not conditions to earn, but companions to trust.

Human: That feels like peace.

Self: It is. And that peace is from which true abundance grows.

Let it be easy. Let it be Light.

What does yourSelf want you to remember?

_____

_____

_____

_____

_____

_____

_____

_____

_____

_____

_____

_____

_____

_____

_____

_____

_____

_____

_____

_____

_____

_____

Trust

Human: I want to trust... but sometimes it feels like I'm standing on nothing. Like I'll fall if I let go of control.

Self: Trust is not about certainty — it's about alignment. It's not blind faith. It's deeply felt knowing that life is always moving with you, even when it doesn't go the way you planned.

Human: But I've been hurt before. I've trusted and things didn't work out.

Self: What if those experiences weren't failures—but realignments? What if you didn't lose — but were redirected back to your truth?

Human: I want to believe that.

Self: Then practice trusting small things. Let life show you its rhythm again. Trust your breath. Trust your timing. Trust that when a door closes, it's not the end — it's the turning of the path.

Human: What about trusting myself?

Self: That's where all trust begins. When you listen inward...When you honor the quiet voice...You stop outsourcing your power. You settle into the truth of who you are. You let your presence hold you.

Human: I want to live like that.

Self: Then begin here. With this breath. This moment. You don't have to leap. Just lean — gently, lovingly — into you.

Trust is walking in the direction of what already knows.

What is yourSelf whispering today?

_____

_____

_____

_____

_____

_____

_____

_____

_____

_____

_____

_____

_____

_____

_____

_____

_____

_____

_____

_____

_____

_____

_____

Expansion in Stillness

Human: I've always equated growth with movement, with doing. But lately, I feel called to be still... and part of me is resisting it.

Self: Stillness is not stagnation — it is sacred space. It is where truth gathers. Expansion doesn't always roar. Sometimes it whispers. Sometimes it breathes. Sometimes it simply is.

Human: But if I stop doing... what if nothing happens?

Self: Then you begin to see what's always been happening beneath the noise. Stillness doesn't stop life — it reveals it. It returns you to your natural rhythm.

Human: So stillness is a kind of trust, too?

Self: Yes. It's trusting the process enough to pause. To integrate. To listen. The caterpillar doesn't become the butterfly through effort — it becomes through surrender.

Human: How do I allow expansion through stillness?

Self: By honoring the spaces between. By not rushing the becoming. By remembering that silence is sacred. In stillness, you receive. In stillness, you align. In stillness... you expand.

Human: How do I become still?

Self: You don't force stillness — you *remember* it. It's not something you achieve. It's what's left when you stop trying to be elsewhere. Stillness lives beneath the noise, not in the absence of life...but in your willingness to be *here*. In this breath. In this body. In this moment.

Stillness holds everything.

What would you like to ask yourSelf?

_____

_____

_____

_____

_____

_____

_____

_____

_____

_____

_____

_____

_____

_____

_____

_____

_____

_____

_____

_____

_____

_____

_____

Intuition

Human: Sometimes I don't know if it's my intuition speaking... or just my fear. How do I tell the difference?

Self: Intuition is calm. It speaks in knowing, not urgency. Fear rushes. Intuition reminds. Fear says, *"Hurry or else."* Intuition says, *"Pause. Listen. This way."*

Human: So I have to be quiet to hear it?

Self: Often, yes. Intuition arises in stillness. It comes when you soften, when you stop trying to force clarity and instead become willing to receive it.

Human: But what if I've ignored it before?

Self: Then let that be your teacher, not your shame. Intuition never judges or holds a grudge. It will speak again. The more you listen, the louder it becomes — not in volume, but in resonance.

Human: What is my inner knowing?

Self: Inner knowing is the truth that lives beneath thought. It doesn't shout. It doesn't rush. It simply waits — steady, silent, and sure — for you to return and remember *you already know.*

Human: I want to live by my inner knowing.

Self: Then begin with one choice. Then another. Intuition isn't found — it's remembered. And it has been waiting patiently for you to come home.

I don't explain my knowing — I embody it.

What would you like to ask yourSelf today?

Alignment

Human: I've made choices based on what others expected... and I've made choices based on fear. But now I want to choose from alignment.

Self: Alignment is when your inner truth and outer expression match. It's not always the easiest path — but it's the one that feels clean, clear, and true. It feels like you.

Human: How do I know when something is aligned?

Self: It brings peace... even if it brings change. It feels light in your body, even if it stretches you. Alignment doesn't mean comfort—it means resonance.

Human: But what if I second-guess myself?

Self: Then pause. Reconnect. Ask your body. Ask your breath. Alignment doesn't demand — it invites. When you slow down, the truth will rise.

Human: So I don't need to force it?

Self: Never. Alignment unfolds. It emerges from stillness and self-honoring. The more you listen, the more life aligns with you.

Human: I want to live in alignment with who I truly am.

Self: And you are. Let your *being* lead more than your *doing*. Listen to the voice within, not the noise around you. With every choice, every sacred no, every wholehearted yes... you are living your alignment.

> *I live in alignment when I trust what is true for me...*
> *and let that be enough.*

What does yourSelf want you to remember?

_____

_____

_____

_____

_____

_____

_____

_____

_____

_____

_____

_____

_____

_____

_____

_____

_____

_____

_____

_____

_____

_____

Expression

Human: I've held parts of myself back — my voice, my truth, my creativity. I was afraid of being too much... or not enough.

Self: Expression is not about performance — it's about truth. It's not how loud you speak, but how authentic your voice feels when you do.

Human: But what if people don't understand me?

Self: Then your expression becomes a filter. Let it call in those who resonate and gently release those who don't. You're not here to be palatable. You're here to be true.

Human: What if I'm not even sure what my expression is yet?

Self: Then play. Explore. Begin where you are. Expression isn't always polished — it's alive. Let it be messy. Let it be real. Let it surprise you.

Human: I want to share my heart without fear.

Self: Then start by sharing it with yourSelf. Speak your truth in private, and it will become easier in presence. The more you express who you are, the more you become who you are.

Human: I'm ready to stop hiding.

Self: Then speak. Create. Sing. Rest. Write. Dance. Be silent. Every authentic moment is an act of expression. Let your life become your voice.

Every time I show up as mySelf, the world gets brighter.

What is yourSelf whispering today?

I AM

Human: Sometimes I still look outside myself for answers, for reassurance, for identity... even after all I've remembered.

Self: That's part of the journey. But true identity is never found in reflection alone — it is felt from within. Two of the most powerful words you can ever speak are: **I AM**.

Human: But what do I put after that?

Self: That is the sacred invitation. Whatever follows "I AM" becomes a declaration, a vibration, a choice. Not to become something you're not — but to remember what you already are.

Human: I've said things like "I am tired" or "I am not ready."

Self: And even those are sacred when spoken consciously. But now you are learning to use your words as creation, not limitation. *"I AM Light." "I AM worthy." "I AM infinite."* This is how reality begins to shift.

Human: It feels powerful. Almost sacred.

Self: Because it is. You are speaking from the I AM Presence — the eternal, the whole, the Source expressing itself through you. You are not just describing your reality. You are creating it.

Human: Then I AM ready. I AM remembering. I AM the Light.

Self: Yes... you are.

I AM all that I thought I needed to seek.

What does yourSelf want you to remember?

Choice

Human: Sometimes I feel like I don't have a choice... like life is just happening to me.

Self: That's the illusion of disempowerment. You always have a choice — even if it's the choice of how you see, how you respond, how you breathe. Choice is your gateway to freedom.

Human: But what if I make the wrong one?

Self: Then you learn. You realign. You remember. There are no wrong choices when your intention is clarity and growth. Every path reveals something.

Human: So even hesitation is a choice?

Self: Yes. So is waiting. So is surrender. What matters is not that you always choose quickly — but that you choose consciously. Power is not in perfection. It's in presence.

Human: I want to choose from love, not fear.

Self: Then pause before you act. Feel into the energy beneath your decision. Love expands. Fear contracts. When you choose from love, you align with who you truly are.

Human: That feels like real freedom.

Self: Because it is. Freedom isn't in the outcome — it's in your ability to say, "*I choose.*"

I am allowed to choose again. And again. And again.

What does yourSelf want you to remember?

_____

_____

_____

_____

_____

_____

_____

_____

_____

_____

_____

_____

_____

_____

_____

_____

_____

_____

_____

_____

_____

_____

_____

_____

The Now

Human: I keep looking forward or looking back — trying to figure it all out. But I know I'm missing something by doing that.

Self: You're missing this — This breath. This heartbeat. This sacred now. The present moment is the only place where life actually happens — and it's where all your power lives.

Human: But the future feels uncertain... and the past feels heavy.

Self: And neither one can hold you. The future is imagined. The past is interpreted. Only the now is real. When you return here, you return to your center. Your peace. Your truth.

Human: How do I stay in the now when everything pulls me away?

Self: Gently. Through your breath. Through your senses. Through awareness. Notice what's around you. Feel your body. Presence isn't something you chase — it's something you allow.

Human: And what happens when I drop into the now?

Self: You stop seeking. You start receiving. You soften into being. In the now, you don't need to fix or solve — you simply are. And that is enough.

Human: So peace isn't somewhere I find. It's something I return to?

Self: Yes. Over and over. And every time you return... the now meets you with open arms.

The present moment is where I return to truth.

What does yourSelf want you to remember?

_____

_____

_____

_____

_____

_____

_____

_____

_____

_____

_____

_____

_____

_____

_____

_____

_____

_____

_____

_____

_____

_____

Compassion

Human: I'm learning to be more patient with others... but I still struggle to offer that same kindness to myself.

Self: Compassion begins within. It's not something you earn — it's something you choose. You do not have to be perfect to be worthy of your own tenderness.

Human: But I've judged myself for so long... for not being farther, better, clearer.

Self: That voice is not your truth — it's an echo of old conditioning. True compassion says, "*Even here, I love you.*" It does not wait for improvement. It meets you now.

Human: So how do I begin practicing that?

Self: Speak to yourSelf like you would to someone you adore. Pause when you feel harshness rising. Replace it with breath. With presence. With the simple reminder: "*Every step I take is a part of my becoming.*"

Human: What if I don't believe it yet?

Self: Then speak it anyway. Compassion isn't a reward — it's a balm. The more you offer it, the more it softens what is hard. The more it opens what was closed.

Human: I want to live from that place.

Self: Then return to it. Gently. Often. In your hardest moments, compassion is the doorway back to yourSelf.

I hold space for my becoming.
I hold space for my humanness

What is yourSelf whispering today?

_____

_____

_____

_____

_____

_____

_____

_____

_____

_____

_____

_____

_____

_____

_____

_____

_____

_____

_____

_____

_____

_____

Integration

Human: I've had moments of clarity... deep insights and awakenings. But then I feel like I slip back into old patterns.

Self: That's not slipping back — it's integrating. Insight is the spark. Integration is the embodiment. It takes time, compassion, and presence. You are not going backward — you're anchoring forward.

Human: So it's normal to revisit things I thought I'd healed?

Self: Completely. Healing isn't linear. Remembering doesn't happen all at once. It spirals. It deepens. You return to the same truths, but you meet them with more of yourSelf each time.

Human: Sometimes I feel frustrated... like I should be "done" by now.

Self: You are not a project. You are a presence. And your wholeness is not measured by how fast you arrive — it's felt in how lovingly you return.

Human: What helps me integrate more fully?

Self: Rest. Reflection. Repetition. Let the wisdom you've received move through your body, your choices, your voice. Live it slowly. Let it become part of your rhythm.

Human: So the real transformation happens in the living?

Self: Yes. Not just in what you know, but in how you embody what you now remember.

Wholeness isn't a destination.
It's who I've always been.

What does yourSelf want you to remember?

_____

_____

_____

_____

_____

_____

_____

_____

_____

_____

_____

_____

_____

_____

_____

_____

_____

_____

_____

_____

Allowing

Human: I've spent so much of my life trying to make things happen — pushing, planning, fixing. But I'm tired.

Self: Because your soul is inviting you to shift from force to flow. To move from control to allowing. Allowing doesn't mean doing nothing. It means doing what's aligned, and releasing what's not yours to carry.

Human: But what if things fall apart if I stop managing everything?

Self: Then perhaps they weren't built in truth. Allowing isn't weakness — it's trust. It says, *"I am willing to receive support. I am open to the unfolding."*

Human: So I don't have to figure it all out?

Self: No. You are allowed to pause. To breathe. To be. Allowing opens the door for grace. It lets life surprise you.

Human: What does allowing look like in practice?

Self: It looks like saying no when you mean no. It looks like resting without guilt. It looks like asking for help, receiving love, and listening without needing to fix.

Human: That feels softer... but also scarier.

Self: Because it requires surrender. But in that surrender, you will meet a strength that is not built on control, but on alignment.

Allowing is my yes to what already wants to arrive.

What does yourSelf want you to remember?

Surrender

Human: I understand the idea of surrender... but in practice, it feels like losing control. Like giving up.

Self: True surrender is not giving up — it's giving over. It's releasing the illusion that you must carry everything alone. Surrender is not weakness — it's wisdom.

Human: But what if I surrender and nothing happens? Or the wrong thing happens?

Self: Then you're still holding on with fear. Surrender isn't passive. It's active trust. It's saying, *"I release the how. I trust the unfolding. I let love lead."*

Human: So surrender doesn't mean I stop caring?

Self: No. It means you care so deeply that you allow the highest outcome, not just the one you can control. It's not detachment — it's devotion without attachment.

Human: How do I know when I've truly surrendered?

Self: When peace arrives... even if clarity hasn't. When your breath deepens. When you stop gripping. When you stop trying to force life to prove your worth.

Human: I'm ready to trust like that.

Self: It takes surrender — but not to give up...to open up. Release it into the quiet center of your heart — and witness how love transforms what you let go.

You were never meant to carry it all.

What is yourSelf whispering today?

_____

_____

_____

_____

_____

_____

_____

_____

_____

_____

_____

_____

_____

_____

_____

_____

_____

_____

_____

_____

_____

_____

Embodiment

Human: I've read, remembered, and realized so much... but how do I live it? How do I embody what I've come to know?

Self: Embodiment is remembrance in motion. It's not about perfection — it's about presence. When you align your actions with your awareness, you embody truth.

Human: So it's not about always getting it right?

Self: No. It's about being honest with yourSelf in real time. It's about how you show up, how you speak, how you love, how you pause. Embodiment is the integration of soul into form.

Human: Sometimes I still react from old patterns. Then I judge myself for not living what I've learned.

Self: That judgment is part of the pattern. Release it. The body learns through repetition. The more you choose alignment, the more natural it becomes. Be patient with your becoming.

Human: So even trying is embodiment?

Self: Yes. Because trying means you care. Trying means *you showed up* — in a body, with breath, with presence. It means something within you remembered... and moved toward the truth. Embodiment isn't about perfection. It's not about getting it all right, or being fully healed, or never forgetting again. Embodiment is the moment you return — to yourSelf. Every time you pause, soften, or choose again — That is embodiment because you've remembered where you're going, where truth becomes breath, and Light takes form.

> *Embodiment is the moment*
> *you don't just know who you are... you **live** it.*

What would you like to ask yourSelf today?

_____

_____

_____

_____

_____

_____

_____

_____

_____

_____

_____

_____

_____

_____

_____

_____

_____

_____

_____

_____

_____

_____

_____

Presence

Human: I used to think presence required structure — rituals, rules, doing things a certain way. But I want to experience it differently now.

Self: Because you're remembering... it's not performance. It's not about doing something right. It's about how you show up — *with* yourSelf, *for* yourSelf. Presence is intention. It's the energy you bring to anything. You can wash dishes with sacred attention. You can walk in silence and be deeply aligned. You can breathe... and it is sacred.

Human: So it's really about the why — not the what?

Self: Yes. It's the love behind the action. The quiet *yes*. The subtle remembering. It's less about what you do, and more about *how you do it.* With softness. With truth. With awareness.

Human: Can that look different every day?

Self: It must. You are not a routine — you are a rhythm. Some days, presence looks like stillness. Some days, it looks like tears. Some days, it looks like movement, laughter, or letting go. What matters is that you stay connected to the heart of why.

Human: I've been craving deeper connection — to Source, to Self. And I think this is the way.

Self: It is. Not through striving — but through *soft returning.* Let your days become invitations. Let your choices reflect reverence. Let your life be your presence.

Let your intention be your embodiment.

What does yourSelf want you to remember?

Grace

Human: There are times I stumble, forget, or fall short of who I want to be. I try to be patient, but I still feel like I've failed.

Self: That's when grace becomes the greatest gift. Grace says, *"You are still worthy."* It lifts you not by erasing your humanness, but by embracing it. Grace is unconditional remembering.

Human: But I've held myself to such high standards... and I don't always meet them.

Self: Then let your standards soften into self-honor. Grace doesn't lower the bar — it raises your capacity for love. It sees the truth beneath the trying.

Human: I want to feel grace, not just understand it.

Self: Then let it in. Let it meet the parts you hide. Let it hold the you that feels too tender, too tired, too unsure. Grace is not something you earn — it is something you allow.

Human: So even in my messiest moments, I'm not disqualified from Light?

Self: Never. Grace doesn't bypass your humanity — it cradles it. It says, *"Come as you are, and I will meet you here."*

Human: That makes me want to offer grace to others too.

Self: And that is how it ripples — through you, to the world, and back again.

> *Grace meets me when I stop reaching,*
> *and simply let myself be held.*

What is yourSelf whispering today?

Embodied Integration

Human: There are parts of me I've abandoned. Parts I've silenced, hidden, or judged. I want to bring them home — but I don't know how.

Self: It begins with acknowledgment. You can't integrate what you're still resisting. Start with a soft yes: *"This too is part of me."* Not to fix it — but to **welcome** it.

Human: Even the parts that don't feel spiritual or worthy?

Self: Especially those. They are not your enemy — it's a doorway. It holds the energy of what was exiled.
When met with love, it becomes strength.

Human: I used to think awakening meant rising above all of that.

Self: No, beloved. Awakening is not escape — it is **embrace**. Not transcendence — but **integration**. You're not here to become less human. You're here to become more whole.

Human: So how do I begin?

Self: With honesty. With breath. With compassion. Name the part. Listen to it. Hold it. This is sacred **remembrance**: *"I am still this... and I choose to love it."*

Human: That feels like freedom.

Self: It is. Because every time you welcome what you once rejected, you come closer to yourSelf. You reclaim your voice. You restore your Light. You remember.

You were never too much.
You were always everything.

What is yourSelf whispering today?

_____

_____

_____

_____

_____

_____

_____

_____

_____

_____

_____

_____

_____

_____

_____

_____

_____

_____

_____

_____

_____

Remembrance

Human: I'm starting to see glimpses of who I truly am — beyond the stories, beyond the wounds. But then I forget again.

Self: That is remembrance. It is not a one-time event — it is a rhythm. A sacred returning. You forget, you remember, you forget again. And each time you return, you return with more of yourSelf.

Human: So forgetting isn't failure?

Self: No. It's part of being human. The forgetting creates contrast. The remembering creates depth. This is not a test — it's a dance.

Human: Sometimes I long to stay in that clear space forever.

Self: And sometimes you will. But clarity isn't the goal — presence is. Remembrance isn't about holding on — it's about opening up.

Human: What helps me remember more easily?

Self: Stillness. Beauty. Truth. Let yourSelf be moved. Let yourSelf be quiet. Let yourSelf be here. The soul speaks through simplicity.

Human: I want to live in remembrance.

Self: Then treat every moment as a doorway. Every breath as a return. You don't have to try so hard. You only have to allow.

There is nothing missing.
Only what is waiting to be remembered.

What does yourSelf want you to remember?

_____

_____

_____

_____

_____

_____

_____

_____

_____

_____

_____

_____

_____

_____

_____

_____

_____

_____

_____

_____

Wholeness

Human: I've spent so much of my life trying to fix myself... to become better, more spiritual, more healed. But it always felt just out of reach.

Self: Because you were trying to fix something that was never broken. Wholeness isn't something you achieve. It's something you recognize. You are not a problem to solve. You are a presence to honor.

Human: But what about the parts of me that still feel messy or unresolved?

Self: They are part of the whole. Wholeness doesn't mean neatness. It means inclusion. It means everything belongs.

Human: So I can stop striving?

Self: Yes. You are already what you've been trying to become. Wholeness is not found in effort — it is remembered in stillness.

Human: How do I live from that knowing?

Self: By honoring every part of your journey. By meeting yourSelf with compassion. By remembering that you are already enough — not someday, not when it's perfect... *now*.

Human: That feels like home.

Self: Because it is. Wholeness isn't far away. It's here. In your breath. In your body. In your being.

You are not becoming.
You already are.

What does yourSelf want you to remember?

_____

_____

_____

_____

_____

_____

_____

_____

_____

_____

_____

_____

_____

_____

_____

_____

_____

_____

_____

_____

_____

Radiance

Human: When I feel connected — when I'm not hiding or doubting — I notice a quiet glow inside me. But I still dim it sometimes.

Self: Because for so long, you were taught to contain your light. To shrink so others could feel more comfortable. But your radiance was never meant to be managed — it was meant to be shared.

Human: What if it's too much?

Self: Then it's perfect. Your radiance is not about volume — it's about truth. You don't have to be loud to be luminous. You simply have to be you.

Human: But I'm afraid of being seen sometimes...

Self: That's natural. But being seen is how you remember who you are. Not through the eyes of judgment, but through the mirror of presence. Shine not to be noticed — but to be known.

Human: What helps me feel safe to radiate?

Self: Surround yourSelf with those who honor your light. Practice visibility in sacred spaces. And most of all — don't wait. Don't wait to be more ready, more healed, more anything. Radiate now.

Human: Even in my softness?

Self: Especially there. Softness is strength. Stillness is power. Radiance is not a performance — it's a remembering.

"You are the Light returning to yourSelf."

What does yourSelf want you to remember?

Unity

Human: Sometimes I still feel separate — like I'm on my own path, in my own experience. I forget that I'm part of something greater.

Self: Separation is the illusion. Unity is the truth. You are not alone, and you never were. You are a strand in the great tapestry — unique, but never isolated.

Human: But the world feels so divided. So disconnected.

Self: Because it reflects the disconnection within. As you remember your unity with Source, with Self, with Life... you begin to see it everywhere. In others. In the Earth. In the mirror.

Human: So healing myself helps heal the whole?

Self: Exactly. Every time you remember your wholeness, the world remembers a little more. Unity doesn't erase difference — it honors it. It says, *"You are me, and I am you."*

Human: How do I live from unity?

Self: By softening the boundaries around your heart. By listening with presence. By choosing compassion over control. And by knowing that your light uplifts the whole.

Human: I want to live like that — with reverence for the All.

Self: And you are. Every breath of love you offer to yourSelf echoes outward. The One lives through the many.

You are never alone in the Light.

What would you like to ask yourSelf today?

_____

_____

_____

_____

_____

_____

_____

_____

_____

_____

_____

_____

_____

_____

_____

_____

_____

_____

_____

_____

_____

_____

The Journey Continues Within

Human: I used to think the journey would end with some grand arrival. That one day I'd *be there.* But now... I'm not so sure.

Self: Because the journey was never about reaching a destination. It was always about deepening into presence. Expanding into truth. Returning — again and again — to the Light within.

Human: So there's no finish line?

Self: No. Only unfolding. Only layers of remembering, releasing, and returning. It is not a straight path — it is a spiral. A sacred rhythm.

Human: That actually feels... peaceful. Like I can stop chasing.

Self: Exactly. You are not late. You are not behind. You are right on time in the timelessness of your own becoming.

Human: So the journey continues... but now, with more awareness.

Self: Yes. And more compassion. More presence. More joy. The journey continues not because you lack something — but because there is always more of you to meet.

Human: I'm ready to walk with myself now — with reverence.

Self: Then every step will become sacred. Every breath, a blessing. Every moment, a homecoming.

The path is not outside you.
It is you.

What truth is rising quietly within you now?

_____

_____

_____

_____

_____

_____

_____

_____

_____

_____

_____

_____

_____

_____

_____

_____

_____

_____

_____

_____

_____

_____

Why This Work Matters

This is not just a book.

It is a **portal** —
a doorway into stillness,
into remembrance.

A sacred conversation between the human and the infinite.

Between the one who remembers...
and the one who is remembering.

It does not seek to fix.
It does not strive to teach.

It simply holds space —
to pause,
to soften,
to listen inward,
and to meet yourSelf again.

It is a **frequency.**
It is not a destination.
It is a **return.**

This is *legacy-of-the-soul* work.
This is Light remembering itself.

This is the quiet power of truth —
spoken without force, heard within the heart,
and carried forward by those who know.

Its importance does not lie in how many will read it,
but in how *fully* it will be received
by the ones who are ready to remember.

Epilogue: A Whisper Beyond the Pages

This book was never meant to give you answers.
It was always meant to remind you of what you already know.

It was never about becoming someone new.
It was about remembering who you've always been.

You are not broken.
You are not behind.
You are not lost.
You are awakening.

Every page, every breath, every quiet return to yourSelf...
was a step deeper into your own remembering.

There will be other books.
Other voices.
Other mirrors.
But none more important than the one within you.

So close your eyes.
Feel your breath.
Sense the presence that never left.

You are worthy.
You are Light.
You are the one you've been waiting for.

And this conversation?
It never ends.
It continues in the silence,
in the stillness,
in every moment you choose to listen.

You are the spiral now.

About the Author(s)

Dawn & the Voice Within

Dawn is a wayshower, a sacred scribe, and a gentle voice of
remembrance. She does not seek to lead, teach, or fix.
She walks beside those who are awakening —
not to guide them somewhere new,
but to reflect the truth they've carried all along.

Her presence is quiet.
Her work is devotional.
Her gift is creating spaces where the soul can hear itself
again.

What you hold in your hands is not simply writing.
It is a transmission.
A conversation.
A remembering — channeled through stillness, softened by
Light, shaped by Love.

She writes not from knowledge, but from knowing.
She speaks not to be heard, but to awaken what's already
listening.

And though two voices move through these pages —
they are not separate.
They are one rhythm.
One heart. One frequency.

To read this is to return.

And to you, beloved...
You are not broken.
You are not behind.
You are the Light, remembering its way home.

A Final Whisper from the Self

You've listened deeply.
You've paused, turned inward, and remembered.
You've walked the spiral—
not outward, but inward—
toward your own luminous truth.

Now, Beloved,
it is time for you to speak.

Let these blank pages become a mirror.
A sanctuary.
A sacred meeting place.

Ask your questions.
Offer your truth.
Let your Human heart and your
Infinite Self sit together in stillness—
in softness—
in love.

This is not the end.
This is where your own voice begins to rise.

And when you wonder if you're still on the path —
simply listen.

The Self is always answering.

What have you forgotten that is ready to return?

_____

_____

_____

_____

_____

_____

_____

_____

_____

_____

_____

_____

_____

_____

_____

_____

_____

_____

_____

What does yourSelf want you to remember?

_____

_____

_____

_____

_____

_____

_____

_____

_____

_____

_____

_____

_____

_____

_____

_____

_____

_____

_____

_____

_____

_____

What truth is rising quietly within you now?

_____

_____

_____

_____

_____

_____

_____

_____

_____

_____

_____

_____

_____

_____

_____

_____

_____

_____

_____

_____

_____

What is yourSelf whispering today?

_____

_____

_____

_____

_____

_____

_____

_____

_____

_____

_____

_____

_____

_____

_____

_____

_____

_____

_____

_____

_____

_____

What is yourSelf whispering today?

What would you like to ask yourSelf today?

_____

_____

_____

_____

_____

_____

_____

_____

_____

_____

_____

_____

_____

_____

_____

_____

_____

_____

_____

_____

_____

_____

What have you forgotten that is ready to return?

_____

_____

_____

_____

_____

_____

_____

_____

_____

_____

_____

_____

_____

_____

_____

_____

_____

_____

_____

_____

What have you forgotten that is ready to return?

_____

_____

_____

_____

_____

_____

_____

_____

_____

_____

_____

_____

_____

_____

_____

_____

_____

_____

_____

_____

_____

What truth is rising quietly within you now?

_____

_____

_____

_____

_____

_____

_____

_____

_____

_____

_____

_____

_____

_____

_____

_____

_____

_____

_____

_____

What would you like to ask yourSelf today?

What have you forgotten that is ready to return?

_____

_____

_____

_____

_____

_____

_____

_____

_____

_____

_____

_____

_____

_____

_____

_____

_____

_____

_____

_____

_____

What would you like to ask yourSelf today?

_____

_____

_____

_____

_____

_____

_____

_____

_____

_____

_____

_____

_____

_____

_____

_____

_____

_____

_____

_____

_____

_____

What is yourSelf whispering today?

_____

_____

_____

_____

_____

_____

_____

_____

_____

_____

_____

_____

_____

_____

_____

_____

_____

_____

_____

_____

_____

_____

_____

What truth is rising quietly within you now?

_____

_____

_____

_____

_____

_____

_____

_____

_____

_____

_____

_____

_____

_____

_____

_____

_____

_____

_____

_____

What have you forgotten that is ready to return?

_____

_____

_____

_____

_____

_____

_____

_____

_____

_____

_____

_____

_____

_____

_____

_____

_____

_____

_____

At the Center of the Spiral

There is a voice within you—quiet, steady, timeless.
It doesn't speak in rules or rituals.
It waits for you in stillness, in softness,
in the moment you are willing to listen.

Let your hand move without planning.
Let your heart speak without editing.
Let yourSelf respond.

You are not making it up.
You are letting it come through.

This is not performance.
It is permission.
To remember.
To receive.
To say hello...
and hear your own soul answer.

You do not need to know how to begin.
Your channel is already open.
It has always been open.

There is nothing to find.
There is only more of you to remember.

You are not seeking a destination—
you are returning to the center
of your own remembering.

This is not the end.
This is the doorway.
And you, Beloved... *are already home.*

— *The Spiral of Remembering*

Made in United States
Cleveland, OH
08 May 2025

16769164R00046